ATOS Book Level: _____1.9_____
AR Points: _____0.5_____
Quiz #: __61692__ ☑RP ☐ LS ☐ VP
Lexile: _____

A Look at Cuba

by Helen Frost

Consulting Editor: Gail Saunders-Smith, Ph.D.

Consultant: Jaime Suchlicki, Ph.D.
Emilio Bacardi Professor of History
Director, Institute for Cuban and Cuban-American Studies
University of Miami

Pebble Books

an imprint of Capstone Press
Mankato, Minnesota

Pebble Books are published by Capstone Press
151 Good Counsel Drive, P.O. Box 669, Mankato, Minnesota 56002
http://www.capstone-press.com

1 2 3 4 5 6 07 06 05 04 03 02

Library of Congress Cataloging-in-Publication Data
Frost, Helen, 1949–
    A look at Cuba / by Helen Frost.
    p. cm.—(Our world)
    Includes bibliographical references and index.
    Contents: Cuba's land—Cuba's animals—Cuba's people—Mogotes—
Map—Flag.
    ISBN 0-7368-1428-0 (hardcover)
    ISBN 0-7368-9388-1 (paperback)
    1. Cuba—Juvenile literature. [1. Cuba.] I. Title. II. Series.
F1758.5 .F76 2003
972.91—dc21   2001007715

Summary: Simple text and photographs depict the land, animals, and people of Cuba.

Note to Parents and Teachers

The Our World series supports national social studies standards related to culture. This book describes and illustrates the land, animals, and people of Cuba. The images support early readers in understanding the text. The repetition of words and phrases helps early readers learn new words. This book also introduces early readers to subject-specific vocabulary words, which are defined in the Words to Know section. Early readers may need assistance to read some words and to use the Table of Contents, Words to Know, Read More, Internet Sites, and Index/Word List sections of the book.

Table of Contents

Havana

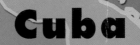

Cuba

N
W ← → E
S

Cuba is a country in the Caribbean Sea. Cuba has one large island and many small islands. The capital of Cuba is Havana.

Cuba's flag

plains

beach

forest

mountains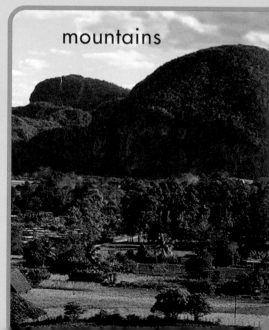

6

Cuba has plains, beaches, forests, and mountains. Cuba is warm most of the year.

Colorful fish swim
in the ocean around
Cuba. Crocodiles live
in Cuba's rivers and marshes.

More than 11 million
people live in Cuba.
Many Cubans live
in Havana. Cubans
speak Spanish.

Many Cubans enjoy music and dancing. Cuban musicians often play African instruments.

Baseball is Cuba's national sport. Many Cubans like boxing and basketball. They also enjoy games like chess and dominoes.

Cuban farms grow tobacco, sugarcane, and vegetables. Some Cubans guide tourists to earn money.

Cuba's money is counted in pesos.

18

Most Cubans travel by
bus, bicycle, and truck.
Some large trucks can
carry 100 people.

Mogotes are mountains found only in Cuba. They have straight sides and a flat top. Some mogotes have caves inside them.

Words to Know

capital—the city in a country where the government is based

Caribbean Sea—a sea near the Atlantic Ocean; Cuba is the largest island in the Caribbean Sea.

Cuba—a country south of the U.S. state of Florida; Cuba consists of one large island and about 1,600 smaller islands.

guide—to show someone around a place or area

island—a piece of land that is surrounded by water

marsh—an area of land that is low and wet

mogote—a large mountain with a flat top; mogotes are several million years old.

sugarcane—a tall, tropical grass that has sugar in its woody stems

tobacco—a plant with large leaves that are harvested and dried in the sun; Cuban workers roll tobacco leaves into cigars.

Read More

Ancona, George. *Cuban Kids.* New York: Marshall Cavendish, 2000.

Petersen, Christine, and David Petersen. *Cuba.* A True Book. New York: Children's Press, 2001.

Schreier, Alta. *Cuba.* A Visit To. Chicago: Heinemann Library, 2001.

Stevens, Kathryn. *Cuba.* Faces and Places. Chanhassen, Minn.: Child's World, 2002.

Internet Sites

Cuba
http://cubanet.net/info.htm

Cuban Flag Quiz/Printout
http://www.enchantedlearning.com/ northamerica/cuba/flag/flagquizbw.shtml

Lonely Planet: Cuba
http://www.lonelyplanet.com/ destinations/caribbean/cuba

Index/Word List

Word Count: 149
Early-Intervention Level: 17

Editorial Credits

Mari C. Schuh, editor; Kia Adams, series designer; Jennifer Schonborn and Patrick D. Dentinger, book designers; Alta Schaffer, photo researcher

Photo Credits

Aurora/Jose Azel, 14; Robert Caputo, 20
Corbis/Tom Brakefield, 8 (bottom)
Jaime Suchlicki, 17 (bill)
Jan Butchofsky-Houser/Houserstock, 1, 6 (upper right), 12, 16
Jay Ireland & Georgienne E. Bradley/BradleyIreland.com, 8 (top)
One Mile Up, Inc., 5
Photri-Microstock/Brent Winebrenner, 10
Trip/T. Bognar, 6 (upper left and lower right); K. McLaren, 18
Visuals Unlimited/Mark Newman, 6 (lower left)
www.danheller.com, cover

A Look at Cuba

by Helen Frost

Consulting Editor: Gail Saunders-Smith, Ph.D.

Consultant: Jaime Suchlicki, Ph.D.
Emilio Bacardi Professor of History
Director, Institute for Cuban and Cuban-American Studies
University of Miami

Pebble Books

an imprint of Capstone Press
Mankato, Minnesota

Pebble Books are published by Capstone Press
151 Good Counsel Drive, P.O. Box 669, Mankato, Minnesota 56002
http://www.capstone-press.com

1 2 3 4 5 6 07 06 05 04 03 02

Library of Congress Cataloging-in-Publication Data
Frost, Helen, 1949–
    A look at Cuba / by Helen Frost.
    p. cm.—(Our world)
    Includes bibliographical references and index.
    Contents: Cuba's land—Cuba's animals—Cuba's people—Mogotes—
Map—Flag.
    ISBN 0-7368-1428-0 (hardcover)
    ISBN 0-7368-9388-1 (paperback)
    1. Cuba—Juvenile literature. [1. Cuba.] I. Title. II. Series.
F1758.5 .F76 2003
972.91—dc21   2001007715

Summary: Simple text and photographs depict the land, animals, and people
of Cuba.

Note to Parents and Teachers

The Our World series supports national social studies standards
related to culture. This book describes and illustrates the land,
animals, and people of Cuba. The images support early readers
in understanding the text. The repetition of words and phrases
helps early readers learn new words. This book also introduces
early readers to subject-specific vocabulary words, which are
defined in the Words to Know section. Early readers may need
assistance to read some words and to use the Table of Contents,
Words to Know, Read More, Internet Sites, and Index/Word List
sections of the book.